FROM FUDGE TO FREEDOM

From Sweet Treats to Healthy Eats

Tips on how to transition to a low-Carb healthy lifestyle.

BY DIANA RICHARDS GOLDEN

Archway Publishing books may be ordered through booksellers or by contacting:

Archway Publishing
1663 Liberty Drive
Bloomington, IN 47403
www.archwaypublishing.com
1 (888) 242-5904

Because of the dynamic nature of the Internet, any web addresses or links contained in this book may have changed since publication and may no longer be valid. The views expressed in this work are solely those of the author and do not necessarily reflect the views of the publisher, and the publisher hereby disclaims any responsibility for them.

Any people depicted in stock imagery provided by Getty Images are models, and such images are being used for illustrative purposes only.
Certain stock imagery © Getty Images.

ISBN: 978-1-4808-6446-7 (sc)
ISBN: 978-1-4808-6445-0 (e)

Library of Congress Control Number: 2018951115

Print information available on the last page.

Archway Publishing rev. date: 09/04/2018

A special thanks to Kathy Pitts for encouraging me to
write this book and giving me the perfect title.

Thank you to all those who supported me through this entire journey.

Contents

Chapter 1: How it all started - Fudge

My first experience with fudge was when I was about 12 years old. My sister, Heidi, would make fudge for her friends as Christmas presents. I helped her make fudge, and we were pretty good at it. Ever since that year, I have made fudge for Christmas. But I got bored with just plain chocolate fudge. I started thinking, "What if I use mint chips, or butterscotch?" Soon I was making all kinds of different flavors. There was no limit...only what I could imagine.

I want to share those recipes in this book. I am only going to include recipes that I have made. I don't want to include recipes I haven't tried yet as I don't have personal experience with them. First, I'll just put the base recipe for all my fudge, then I will include ALL the varieties and how to alter the base recipe.

Fudge

Ingredients:

Variety Fudge plate

- ¾ Cup Butter/Margarine (1 ½ sticks)
- ⅔ Cup or 5 oz. can Evaporated Milk
- 3 Cups Sugar (white)
- 1 (7oz) Marshmallow Cream
- 3 Cups (or 1 ½ pkg) of Chocolate Chips
- *I use 2 pkg (or 4 Cups) for single batch
- 1 teaspoon Vanilla

Directions:

Melt margarine, add evaporated milk & sugar. Bring to a rolling boil. Keep at a rolling boil about 5 minutes. Put a drop in cold water to form a soft ball. Once you can form a soft ball it is ready. Remove from heat. Add marshmallow cream & vanilla. Stir until marshmallow cream is melted. Add chocolate chips and stir until melted. Put in greased/sprayed cake pan 9x13. Cool in fridge or freezer.

When using flavoring, add 1 Tablespoon after everything is melted and mixed together.

For recipes using Torani syrup, you can use 1 Tablespoon of flavoring instead for better results. I find most flavors are available at a specialty store such as Orson Gygi.

If doing a double batch, use a 12x18 baking sheet or lasagna pan.

Blackberry Lemonade Fudge

Use White chips.

Once chips are melted, add 1 Tablespoon Lemon Flavoring. Put in pan, and pour ½ - 1 Cup Torani Blackberry syrup and swirl with a knife or spoon through the fudge mixture.

Butterscotch Fudge

Use Butterscotch chips.

Caramel Apple Fudge

(Two options for this variety)

Option 1:

Add 4 Tablespoons Apple flavoring to the chocolate fudge.

Melt 1 pkg (or 2 cups) caramel bits or squares.

8 oz unsweetened apple rings. Chop into small pieces and mix with the melted caramel.

Once chocolate is in the pan, add caramel & apple layer.

Caramel Apple Fudge

Option 2:

Use green chips. Add 4 Tablespoons Apple flavoring to the green chips.

Melt 1 pkg (or 2 cups) caramels.

Swirl caramel to green fudge once it is in the pan.

Chocolate Orange Fudge

Add 1 Tablespoon Orange flavoring.

Once fudge is cooled, top with the zest of 1 orange.

Citrus Fudge

Use white chips.

- 1 Tablespoon Lemon flavoring
- 1 Tablespoon Lime flavoring

Add zest of 1 lemon & 1 lime to top.

Citrus Fudge

Cookies 'N Cream/ Mint Oreo Fudge

Use white chips. Add 1 pkg crushed Oreos after everything is melted.

Use Green mint chips, and 1 pkg Oreos for Mint Oreo.

Mint Oreo Fudge

Dark Chocolate Cherry Fudge

Option 1: Use Dark Chocolate chips and 1 Cup chopped dried cherries.

Option 2: Make a single batch of dark chocolate chips & a single batch of cherry chips.

Swirl together.

Chocolate Cherry Swirl Fudge

Mint Explosion Fudge

(Two options for making this variety)

Option 1: Use Andes Mint chips. Make a double batch (3 pkg or 6 Cups chips).

Once everything is melted, let fudge cool about 5 minutes before adding 1 pkg (or 4 Cups) Mint Cookie Bites. Put in greased pan & cool.

Mint Explosion Fudge

Option 2: Use Green Mint chips.

Add 2 – 2 ½ Cups Mint Cookie Bites

For single batch 2 pkg chips and 2 – 2 ½ Cups Cookie Bites

For double batch 3 pkg chips & 4 ½ - 5 Cups Cookie Bites

Let fudge cool 5 – 10 minutes before adding the cookie bites.

Mint swirl Fudge

Use green mint chips.

Make a second batch of fudge with chocolate base. Use some of the chocolate fudge to swirl into the green mint.

Mint swirl Fudge

Oranges 'N Cream Fudge

Make a single batch using white chips and a single batch using orange chips with 1 Tablespoon Orange flavoring. Swirl together after both are completely made, but still warm.

Be creative. You can do this with Strawberry, Raspberry, or any fruit flavor & colored chips.

Oranges 'N Cream Fudge

Peach/Mango Fudge

Use white chips, and 1-2 Cups Peach/Mango Smoothie mix.

Make consistency into a hard ball. Add smoothie mix to taste.

Peanut Butter Cup Fudge

Use a single batch of chocolate. Use peanut butter chips for single batch. Add peanut butter fudge after chocolate layer has cooled a bit.

PB Cup Fudge

Raspberry Salted Caramel

Use Salted Caramel chips. Add 1 Tablespoon Raspberry flavoring. Drop red food coloring on top and swirl.

Peppermint Bark Fudge

Make a single batch of chocolate for bottom layer.

Raspberry Salted Caramel Fudge

For peppermint layer you have two options:

1) Use white chips with 1 Tablespoon Peppermint flavoring, and add 2 Cups chopped candy canes.
2) Use Andes peppermint chips

Rocky Road Fudge

Use chocolate chips. Once chips are melted, add 1 Cup chopped nuts (pecans, cashews, macadamia nuts, your choice).

Let fudge with nuts cool about 5 minutes before adding 1 Cup mini marshmallows.

S'mores Fudge

Use chocolate chips.

Add 1 Cup crushed graham crackers.

Let fudge & crackers cool 5 minutes before adding 1 Cup mini marshmallows

Samoan Turtle Fudge

Use chocolate chips.

Samoan Turtle

- 1 Cup coconut syrup (Torani) or 1 Tablespoon Coconut flavoring
- 1 Cup chopped macadamia nuts
- 2 Cups melted caramels (melt in microwave with 1 Tablespoon Evaporated milk)

Add Coconut syrup/flavoring & macadamia nuts after all is melted and mixed. Swirl melted caramel on after fudge is in the pan.

Toffee/Caramel Fudge

Use chocolate chips.

- 1 pkg toffee chips
- ½ jar Mrs. Richardson's Butterscotch/Caramel topping, or melt 1 pkg (2 Cups) caramel bits.

Add toffee chips and swirl in the caramel.

Chapter 2: Branching Out - Pies

I started branching out with my baking. I wanted to see if I was good at making other types of desserts. I was inspired by Marie Callender's pies. I thought that if I could make my own pies maybe I could save some money, as pies can be expensive for a poor college student. It started with just pudding & whipped topping. Over time I have created a fabulous Triple Chocolate Pie, and discovered a base pie recipe for any flavor of juice or Jell-O.

I want to start with my original pie recipes. Then all the varieties of pies I know. Now, I am all about simplicity. I don't make my own pie crusts. I just buy them. Mostly I use graham cracker crusts, but there are some I use Oreo crusts, and some I prefer with shortbread or Nilla wafers.

Banana Cream Pie

- 1 small pkg (3 oz) Banana pudding
- 1 ¾ Cups Milk
- 2-3 bananas
- 1 Graham cracker pie crust
- 1 – 8oz Whipped topping

Make pudding with milk. Line pie crust with sliced bananas. Add more sliced bananas to pudding. Mix ½ container of Whipped topping with pudding mixture. Fill the pie crust with pudding mix. Spread the rest of the Whipped topping on top of the pie. Let cool in the fridge for an hour before serving.

Coconut Cream Pie

- 1 small pkg Vanilla pudding (They have now come out with Coconut Cream Pudding if you want to use that)
- 1 ¾ Cups Milk
- 1 Cup shredded Coconut
- 1 graham cracker crust
- 1 – 8 oz. Whipped topping

Mix pudding & milk. Add shredded coconut, and mix ½ Whipped topping with pudding mixture. Put in pie crust and top with the rest of the Whipped topping. Let set in fridge before serving.

Triple Chocolate Pie

This recipe makes 4 pies.

Triple Layer Chocolate Pie

- 4 Oreo pie crusts
- 1 pkg (or 2 Cups) Dark Chocolate chips – melted with 2 Tablespoons of Milk
- ¼ Cup Softened Butter
- 8 oz. Cream Cheese
- 1 Cup Powdered Sugar
- 1 large pkg (6 oz) Chocolate Pudding (or two 3.9 oz pkg)
- 3 ½ Cups Milk
- 3 - 8 oz. Whipped topping
- 1 large chocolate bar

Melt chocolate chips with 2 Tablespoons milk in a double-boiler or in the microwave 30 seconds at a time. Stir chips every 30 seconds. Spread melted chocolate in each pie crust so each has about the same amount. Put pie crusts in fridge to cool. Make pudding with milk. Set aside. Mix Cream Cheese, Butter, & Powdered Sugar until creamy. Blend mixture & pudding. Add 1 – 8 oz. whipped topping and mix well. Split filling into 4 pie crusts. Top each with ½ container whipped topping. Use potato peeler to peel chocolate shavings onto the top of each pie.

Creamsicle Pie

This recipe makes 2 pies.

- 2 small pkgs (3 oz) Vanilla pudding or 1 large (6 oz) pkg
- 1 - 12 oz Evaporated Milk
- ½ Cup Orange Cream Smoothie mix
- 1 small pkg (3 oz) Orange gelatin (Jell-O)
- 1 Cup Boiling water
- 8 oz Cream Cheese
- 1 Cup Powdered Sugar
- 1 – 8 oz Whipped topping

Creamsicle Pie

Mix evaporated milk & vanilla pudding. Spread half in each pie crust. Make orange Jell-O with boiling water. Mix hot Jell-O, cream cheese, powdered sugar, smoothie mix & Whipped topping in a blender. Pour mixture into pie crusts. Let cool in fridge for about 1 hour before serving.

Peanut Butter Cream Pie

- ½ Cup Creamy Peanut Butter
- 4 oz. Cream Cheese
- 1 Cup Powdered Sugar
- 1 teaspoon Vanilla
- 8 oz. Whipped topping
- Oreo pie crust

Peanut Butter Cream Pie

Cream Cheese, Whipped topping & peanut butter should be room temperature. Mix together until smooth. Blend in Powdered Sugar. Add vanilla. Add Whipped topping & blend well. Pour into pie crust and let cool before serving. Do NOT use fat free products or pie will not set.

Jell-O (Gelatin) Cream Pies (any flavor)

- 1 Pie Crust
- 1 Cup Boiling water
- 1 small pkg (3 oz) Jell-O (gelatin)
- 1 Cup Powdered Sugar
- 4 oz. Cream Cheese
- 8 oz. Whipped topping

Dissolve Jell-O (gelatin) in boiling water. Blend with cream cheese, powdered sugar & Whipped topping. Pour in pie crust and cool about 2 hours before serving.

Peach/Mango Pie

This recipe makes 3 pies.

Use base recipe for Jell-O pie. Just double the recipe because you are using 2 packages of Jell-O.

- 1 small pkg (3 oz) Mango Jell-O
- 1 small pkg (3 oz) Peach Jell-O

Chocolate Raspberry Pie

This recipe makes 2 pies.

Chocolate Raspberry Pie

- ½ pkg (1 Cup) Dark Chocolate chips – melted with 1 Tablespoon milk
- 2 Oreo pie crusts
- 1 small pkg (3 oz) of Raspberry Jell-O.

Melt chocolate chips (with milk) for 30 seconds at a time in the microwave. Stirring at each interval. Spread half of the melted chocolate in each pie crust. Cool pie crusts in the fridge. Make Jell-O pie base recipe with Jell-O. Fill pie crusts and cool about 2 hours before serving.

Liliko'i Mousse Pie (Passion Fruit)

*This is the base recipe for any flavor juice...Guava, Orange/Mango, etc.

- 2 Cups Liliko'i juice (Passion Fruit)
- ½ Cup Sugar
- ¼ Cup Corn Starch
- Keep ¼ Cup Liliko'i juice separate.
- 1 Shortbread (or graham cracker) pie crust
- 1 ¼ Cups Whipping Cream
- ¼ Cup Sugar

1) Bring 1 ¾ Cup juice to a simmer (boiling around the edges).
2) In a bowl mix corn starch & ½ Cup Sugar
3) Take ¼ Cup of simmering juice from the pan. Add it & ¼ Cup cold juice to corn starch & sugar. Mix well.
4) Add mixture to saucepan, stirring over medium heat until thick.
5) Once thick, put it in the fridge & cool completely (about 30 – 60 minutes).
6) Beat ¼ Cup Sugar & Whipping Cream until peaks form.
7) Add whipping cream & cooled Liliko'i base. Mix together until creamy.
8) Put in shortbread or graham cracker pie crust.
9) Let set in fridge & cool before serving.

If you want to make your own pie crust, my recipe for Melting Moments Shortbread Cookies is excellent. (See Index)

Press dough into a pie tin and bake at 375* for 9 – 11 minutes, or until crisp and slightly golden around the edges.

Toll House Cookie Pie

Cookie Pie

- 8-inch unbaked deep dish pie crust & tin
- 2 Eggs
- ½ Cup Flour
- ½ Cup Sugar (white)
- ½ Cup Brown Sugar (packed)
- ¾ Cup Butter (softened to room temperature)
- 1 Cup Chocolate chips (semi-sweet)
- 1 Cup Walnuts *optional

Pre-heat oven to 325*. Line deep dish pie tin with unbaked pie crust, crimping edges.

Beat eggs until light and foamy. Add flour & sugars & mix. Add softened butter & mix. Stir in ½ cup chocolate chips & nuts until evenly spread throughout the batter. Spoon batter into prepared pie crust. Spread the rest of the chocolate chips on top of the batter.

Bake for 50 – 60 minutes or until fork or knife comes out clean.

Let cool on wire rack about 30 minutes. Serve warm with vanilla ice cream & hot fudge or caramel.

Chapter 3: Baking is Addicting

I started doing bake sales at work selling pies and fudge. I would take a whole day off to bake. I remember making about 30 small plates of fudge, and 40 pies for one bake sale. I would make enough money to pay for ingredients and a little extra.

I grew up making cookies and Texas Sheet Cake for family dinners, but now I am a baking fanatic.

I was having so much fun with pies and fudge and thought, "I really have a knack for baking." I started finding all kinds of recipes from friends and co-workers. I found that I was good at making desserts, and I loved it. I have made some amazing, tasty desserts over the years and want to have them all available in this book.

This next section includes a variety of desserts I have made over the years.

3-2-1 Microwave Cake

- 1 Box Angel Food Cake
- 1 Box Chocolate cake (any flavor cake mix)
- 2 Tablespoons Water

Mix two cake mixes together in a gallon Ziploc or other air-tight container.

Take 3 Tablespoons cake mix & 2 Tablespoons water. Mix in mug. Microwave for 1 minute in the microwave. Let stand & serve with toppings.

*This is a fun recipe to make with kids for an activity.

Brownie Fudge Cake

- 1 pkg Fudge Brownie mix & ingredients listed on the box.
- 8 oz. Cream Cheese (softened)
- 1 ½ Cups Powdered Sugar
- 2-8 oz. Whipped topping
- 1 large pkg (6 oz) chocolate pudding
- 2 Cups cold 2% Milk
- 1 pkg toffee bits or crushed Oreos

Pre-heat oven to 350*. Mix and bake brownies as instructed using a 9x13 cake pan. Let cool completely.

In a large mixing bowl, beat cream cheese & powdered sugar until smooth. Fold in 8 oz. whipped topping, and spread over cooled brownies.

In another mixing bowl combine pudding and milk; beat for 2 minutes. Refrigerate for 5 minutes then spread over the cream cheese layer.

Spread the remaining 8 oz. Whipped topping over the top of the pudding. Sprinkle with toffee bits or crushed Oreos. Put in fridge.

Caramel Layer Brownies

- 1 pkg German Chocolate cake mix
- ¾ Cup Butter/Margarine melted
- ⅓ Cup Evaporated Milk
- 1 pkg (2 Cups) Semi-sweet chocolate chips
- 2 Cups Melted Caramels (or 1 pkg caramel bits)

Caramel Layer Brownies

Caramel mix:

- Caramels
- 1/3 Cup evaporated Milk

Melt in microwave 2-3 minutes until smooth when stirred.

Directions:

Pre-heat oven to 350*.

Mix well. Spread and flatten ½ the batter in a 9x13 sprayed/greased cake pan. Bake for 6 minutes.

Sprinkle ½ bag (1 Cup) chocolate chips. Pour caramel over top.

Take remaining batter; flatten & cover the top with flattened batter. It will spread, so don't worry if there are gaps. Bake another 8 minutes.

Sprinkle the remaining chocolate chips (1 Cup) on top.

*Varieties can be made with Raspberry jam or peanut butter. You can use mini muffin tins to make bite size brownies.

Chocolate Mint Brownies

Prepare your favorite brownie mix according to instructions on package. Let brownies cool completely.

Mint filling:

- ½ Cup Softened Butter
- 2 Cups Powdered Sugar
- 1 Tablespoon Water
- ½ teaspoon Mint Extract
- 3 Drops Green food coloring

Topping:

- ½ Cup Semi-Sweet Chocolate Chips
- 1 Tablespoon Butter

Cream butter & Powdered Sugar. Add water, extract & coloring until blended. Spread over cooled brownies.

Refrigerate until set.

Melt chocolate chips & butter. Cool for 5-10 minutes, stirring occasionally. Spread over the filling layer. Chill. Store in fridge.

Ginger/Molasses Cookies

Ginger Cookies

- ½ Cup Butter
- 1 Cup Brown Sugar
- 1 Egg
- ¼ Cup Molasses
- ½ teaspoon Salt
- 2¼ Cups Flour
- 2 teaspoons Baking Soda
- ½ teaspoon Cinnamon
- 1 teaspoon Ginger (I use ginger powder)

Roll into balls and coat with white sugar.

Bake at 375* for 9-10 minutes. You can use silicon baking mats on cookie sheet for more non-stick.

Chocolate Chip/Butterscotch Monster Cookies

This recipe makes about 7-8 dozen large cookies, but you can half the recipe. If making a full batch you need a huge mixing bowl. Only half of the recipe will fit in a Kitchen Aid mixer at one time.

Monster cookies

For softer cookie, you can play around with amount of flour & oats. Reduce by ½ Cup of each.

- 1 lb. Butter, softened
- 3 Cups Sugar (white)
- 3 Cups packed Brown Sugar
- 4 Eggs
- 1 Tablespoon Vanilla
- 5 Cups Oatmeal (regular or quick – no instant). Pulverize oats in a blender. Do not put all five cups in at once.

- 3 Cups Flour (stir before measuring)
- 1 Tablespoon Baking Powder
- 2 teaspoons Salt
- 2 teaspoons Baking Soda
- 1 pkg (or 2 Cups) Chocolate Chips
- 1 pkg (or 2 Cups) Butterscotch Chips
- 3 Cups (Walnuts or pecans) *optional
- 1 (7 - 10 oz) milk chocolate bar, grated

Beat softened butter with electric mixer until light & fluffy. Add sugars & continue beating until fluffy, around 4-5 minutes. Add eggs one at a time, beating well after each one. Add vanilla.

Mix together oats, flour, baking powder, salt & baking soda. With a wooden spoon add wet ingredients. Add chips, nuts*, & grated chocolate. Dough will be very stiff. You may need to use clean hands to incorporate all ingredients.

Preheat oven to 325*. Shape dough into golf ball size. You can use a large cookie scoop. Place on greased cookie sheet.

Bake around 12-16 minutes. Do NOT over bake! If bottom of cookies are lightly brown they are done. Let cookies set a few minutes before removing to cool.

Melting Moments Shortbread Cookies

- 1 Cup Flour
- ½ Cup Cornstarch
- ½ Cup Powdered Sugar
- ¾ Cup Butter (unsalted)
- 1 teaspoon Vanilla

Frosting:

- 3 Cups Powdered Sugar
- ⅓ Cup Butter
- 1-3 Tablespoons Milk
- 1 teaspoon Vanilla (or almond flavoring)
- 2 Tablespoons Cocoa

Soften butter & combine all ingredients. Do NOT melt butter. It should be softened to room temperature.

Cookies do not spread. You can use a cookie press to do shapes.

Bake at 375* for 9-11 minutes.

Let cookies cool before removing from cookie sheet. Cookies will crumble if you try to take them off too soon.

Frosting is enough for a double batch.

Variety options:

Instead of frosting you can dip in melted chocolate or melted Andes mints.

You can also make a glaze with 1 Cup Powdered Sugar and 3 Tablespoons Juice (this makes the flavor of the glaze).

Mrs. Fields Chocolate Chip Cookies

- 1 Cup Butter/Margarine
- 1 ½ Cups Sugar (white)
- 2 Cups packed Brown Sugar
- 3 Eggs
- 2 Tablespoons Vanilla
- 6 Cups Flour
- 1 ½ teaspoons Baking Soda
- ¾ teaspoon Salt
- 1 pkg (or 2 Cups) Chocolate Chips

Beat softened butter, sugars & eggs until fluffy. Add Baking soda, salt & vanilla. Gradually add flour. Add chocolate chips.

Bake at 375* for 12-15 minutes.

For longer lasting soft cookies bake at 325* for 19-20 minutes.

Oreos

- 2 pkg Devil's Food Cake mix
- 4 Eggs
- ⅔ Cup Oil

Frosting:

Red Velvet Oreos

- 8 oz. Cream Cheese
- 1 stick (½ Cup) Butter/Margarine
- 6 Cups Powdered Sugar
- 1 teaspoon Vanilla

Bake at 350* for 8-11 minutes.

Line cookie sheet with wax paper. Use extra small cookie scoop. Makes 80 cookies. Flatten with fork or spoon.

Variety:

Use Red Velvet cake mix for Red Velvet Oreos. Makes about 72 cookies.

Peanut Butter Cup Cookies

Use Hershey's Peanut Butter Cookie mix. Make cookies according to recipe on box. Use greased mini-muffin tins. Fill each spot ½ full of dough.

Use Peanut Butter cups or Rolos or Butterfinger Peanut Butter cups.

Bake at 375* for 7-9 minutes.

PB Cup Cookies

While cookies are baking, unwrap candies. Use two bite size Butterfinger Peanut Butter Cups per cookie. As soon as you pull cookies out of the oven put candy in middle of cookie and push down a little. Let cool before taking out of the pan.

Pumpkin Chocolate Chip Cookies

- 2 boxes Spice cake mix
- 1-29 oz. can Pumpkin
- 1 pkg (or 2 Cups) Semi-sweet Chocolate chips

Mix all ingredients, adding chips last.

Pumpkin Ch. Chip cookies

Bake at 350* for 10-12 minutes.

Dirt

- ¼ Cup Butter softened
- 8 oz. Cream Cheese softened
- 1 Cup Powdered Sugar
- 4 ½ Cups Milk
- 2 small pkgs (3 oz) Chocolate Pudding

Make pudding with milk. In a separate bowl soften butter & cream cheese. Mix with powdered sugar. Mix with pudding. Put in 9x13 cake pan. Add crushed Oreos & gummy worms to top.

Double Chocolate Cake

- 1 pkg Chocolate cake mix
- 1 small pkg (3 oz) chocolate pudding
- 4 Eggs
- ½ Cup Oil
- ½ Cup warm Water
- 1 Cup Sour Cream
- 1 ½ Cups Chocolate chips

Combine all ingredients & beat for 2 minutes. Add chocolate chips and mix well.

Bake at 350* for 50-60 minutes. Make sure bundt pan is greased well.

Frozen Lemon Bars

- 1 small pkg (3 oz) Lemon Jell-O
- 1 Cup boiling Water
- 3 Tablespoons Lemon juice
- 12 oz. can Evaporated Milk
- 1 Cup Sugar (white)
- 1 teaspoon Vanilla
- ½ box Nilla wafers, crushed

Whip Evaporated Milk, Vanilla & Sugar. Make Jell-O (with boiling water).

Mix Jell-O, Lemon juice & whipped ingredients. Put in cake pan. Cover with crushed Nilla wafers. Put in freezer. Serve from frozen.

Fruit Ice Cream

- 2 ¾ Cups Sugar (white)
- ⅓-½ Cup Lemon juice
- 3-4 Cups Chopped/blended fruit
- ½ teaspoon Salt
- 2 - 12 oz. cans Evaporated Milk
- 1 Pint Half & Half
- ½ - 1 Pint Whipping Cream

*Use fresh fruit, or 3 - 10 oz. pkg frozen fruit.

Mix all ingredients in mixing bowl. If you have a Kitchen Aid mixer & ice cream attachment, put ice cream attachment bowl in freezer for at least 6 hours before making ice cream. Put mixing blade in the frozen bowl BEFORE adding mixture. Start the mixer immediately. Mix about 20-30 minutes until you hear the clicking sound. That means the ice cream is thick and ready.

This recipe may be enough for 2 batches. Do Not fill the frozen bowl too high or you won't have room for the mixing blade. If you make more than one batch, you will need to put clean bowl back in the freezer for a few hours.

Mint Chocolate Chip Ice Cream

- 2 Cups Whipping Cream
- 1 Cup Whole Milk
- ¾ Cup Sugar (white)
- ½ teaspoon Mint Extract
- Green Food coloring
- ½ Cup mini-chocolate chips

Mix all ingredients (except chocolate chips). If you have a Kitchen Aid mixer & ice cream attachment, put ice cream attachment bowl in freezer for at least 6 hours before making ice cream. Put mixing blade in the frozen bowl BEFORE adding mixture. Start the mixer immediately. Mix about 20-30 minutes until you hear the clicking sound. That means the ice cream is thick and ready. Add chocolate chips toward the end, about 18 minutes in.

Jell-O Cake

- 6 oz. pkg Jell-O (gelatin) any flavor
- 1 pkg White Cake mix
- 8 oz. Whipped topping

Make White cake according to instructions on the box.

Make Jell-O with boiling water.

While cake is warm, poke holes in the cake and pour warm Jell-O over the cake. Cool in fridge. Once cooled, top with Whipped topping.

Lemon Cake

- 1 pkg Lemon cake mix
- 1 small pkg (3 oz) Lemon (gelatin) Jell-O
- 4 Eggs
- ¾ Cup Oil
- ¾ Cup Water

Lemon Cake

Sauce:

- 2 Cups Powdered Sugar
- ⅓ Cup Lemon juice

Glaze:

- 1 Cup Powdered Sugar
- 3 Tablespoons Lemon juice

Pre-heat oven to 350*. Beat all ingredients together for 4 minutes. Bake in greased & floured bundt pan for 40 minutes. Cool for 10 minutes. Then make the sauce.

Poke holes in cake (before removing from bundt pan) & fill with sauce.

When cake is cool, make the glaze. Remove cake from pan. Drizzle glaze over the top of the cake.

Peanut Butter Brownies

- 2 boxes Brownie mix & ingredients needed to make them.
- 1 pkg (or 2 Cups) Semi-sweet chocolate chips
- 1 pkg (or 2 Cups) Peanut Butter Chips

Make brownies as instructed on the box. Add chips. Put in 12x18 greased Baking Sheet. Bake according to the box for a 9x13 pan, or until fork/toothpick comes out clean. There might be some chips on the fork.

Varieties: Mint chips, Butterscotch chips, any flavor chips can replace the Peanut Butter.

Slutty Brownies

- 1 pkg Brownie Mix & ingredients to make them.
- 1 pkg Oreos
- ½ Cup Butter (unsalted)
- ¼ Cup Brown Sugar
- ¾ Cup White Sugar
- 1 Egg
- 1 ¼ teaspoon Vanilla
- 1 ¼ Cup Flour
- ½ teaspoon Salt
- ½ teaspoon Baking Soda
- ½ teaspoon Baking Powder
- 1 Cup Chocolate Chips
- Caramel ice cream topping or melted caramel bits.

Pre-heat oven to 350*. Spray or grease 9x13 pan liberally.

Prepare brownie mix according to directions on box. Set aside.

For cookie layer, cream butter & sugars. Add egg & vanilla. Add dry ingredients, then chocolate chips.

Gently press cookie dough into bottom of pan. Create an even layer. Add Oreo cookies. Keep close together, but do not overlap cookies. Drizzle caramel sauce over Oreos. Pour prepared brownie mix evenly over the top.

Bake 40-45 minutes, until fork comes out clean. It's ok if there is a little brownie on the fork. Do NOT over-bake the cookie layer.

Once out of the oven drizzle caramel & sprinkle salt over the top.

Cool before serving for easier serving & handling.

Texas Sheet Cake

- 1 Cup Butter/Margarine
- 1 Cup Water
- ¼ Cup Cocoa
- 2 Eggs
- ½ Cup Milk
- 1 Tablespoon Vinegar
- 1 teaspoon Baking Soda
- 1 teaspoon Salt
- 1 teaspoon Vanilla
- 2 Cups Sugar (white)
- 2 Cups Flour

Frosting:

- 1 Cup Butter/Margarine
- ⅓ Cup Milk
- 1 teaspoon Salt
- 3 – 4 Cups Powdered Sugar
- ¼ Cup Cocoa

Pre-heat oven to 325*. Spray or grease 12x18 cookie sheet.

Melt butter/margarine, add water, cocoa, eggs, milk, vinegar, baking soda, salt & sugar. Mix well. Add flour and blend.

Pour mixture into greased pan. Bake for 22-25 minutes.

Make frosting while cake is baking. Consistency should be like lava. If you tilt the bowl it should move slowly. Spread frosting while cake is still warm.

TWIX Salad

TWIX Salad

- 1 small pkg (3 oz) Vanilla pudding
- ¼ Cup Milk
- 16 oz Whipped Topping
- 2 Cups TWIX chopped into bite size pieces
- 3-4 Granny Smith Apples
- Caramel sauce (or 1 package caramel bits melted)

Prepare pudding with ¼ Cup milk. Mix pudding & Whipped Topping. Chop TWIX into bite size pieces. Dice apples. Mix everything. Drizzle caramel sauce over the top. Allow to set in fridge about 30 minutes.

Note: For more tart taste add more apples. For more sweet taste add more TWIX chunks.

Whipper Snap Cookies

This is the **easiest** cookie recipe, and you can be creative for all kinds of varieties.

Whipper Snaps

- 1 pkg Lemon cake mix (or whatever flavor you want for cookies)
- 1 – 8 oz. Whipped topping
- Powdered Sugar

Combine Whipped topping & Cake mix in a bowl. Mix well. It should be thick and sticky consistency. Use extra small cookie scoop or small spoon to drop into powdered sugar & roll into a ball. Make sure it is coated with powdered sugar. Place on greased cookie sheet.

Bake at 350* for 9-11 minutes.

Varieties:

Orangeos

Use orange cake mix. Put orange/Creamsicle frosting on flat side, and put two cookies together to make a cookie with filling.

Glaze

For a glaze to drizzle over cookies (once they're cooled). Use 1 Cup Powdered Sugar & 3 Tablespoons water or juice. Examples; Lemon cake mix, make glaze with 3 Tablespoons lemon juice & 1 Cup Powdered Sugar. Mango cake mix, with mango or passion fruit glaze. Lime cake mix, with lime juice glaze, etc. Be creative.

Frosting

- 3 Cups Powdered Sugar
- ⅓ Cup Butter
- 1-3 Tablespoons Milk
- 1 teaspoon Vanilla (or flavoring)

You can make your own orange frosting using orange flavoring and food coloring.

Chapter 4: Transition from Baking to Cooking

As you can see from all the recipes, I loved making sweet treats. But, I thought I should try cooking real food instead of just sweets all the time. I had some great roommates who were very talented at cooking. I did what I could to pay attention and learn how to be creative and experiment with flavors.

I was pretty good at following a recipe, but when it came to being creative I really missed the mark and had a lot to learn. By the way, just using lemon juice to cook chicken does NOT make a good lemon chicken. I stuck to recipes for a while and found some good ones. I collected recipes from friends and family of foods I had tried and liked.

I was pleasantly surprised that I really had learned a lot just helping my mom cook Sunday dinners around the house. When I got engaged, I remember my first Thanksgiving dinner with my in-laws. They had only had gravy made from a package. I was so excited to contribute to Thanksgiving dinner by making mashed potatoes and gravy, using the turkey drippings. Now, I love spending Thanksgiving with my in-laws and helping prepare the wonderful dinner. I have gotten several of my recipes from my mother-in-law. I would like to share all my other recipes in this chapter. I have not included Low-Carb recipes here as they will be included in the Healthy Recipe section.

Let's start with appetizers and side dishes. Recipes with * can be low-Carb if you watch your serving size.

Biscuits & Gravy

Pillsbury biscuits. Bake as directed.

Gravy:

- 1 lb Sausage
- Milk
- Flour
- Garlic Salt
- All-season Salt
- Pepper

Brown the sausage in a large (12 inch) skillet. Once browned, add flour to soak up the grease. Add milk to hot pan (almost to the top of the skillet). Stir until thick.

Add seasons to taste. Pour over cooked biscuits and enjoy!

Brazilian Lemonade

- 4 Juicy Limes (thin skin)
- 6 Cups Cold Water
- 1 Cup Sugar
- 6 Tablespoons Sweetened Condensed Milk

Directions:

1) Mix cold water & sugar very well, and chill until ready to use. This step can be done ahead of time.
2) Wash limes thoroughly with soap to get wax & pesticides off. You are using the whole lime. Cut the ends off each lime & cut into 8 pieces.
3) Place ½ of limes in blender.
4) Add ½ of the sugar & water, place the lid on the blender & pulse 5 times (Blendtec). Place a fine mesh strainer over a pitcher (the pitcher you'll serve lemonade in) and pour the blended mixture through the strainer & into the pitcher. Use a spoon to press the rest of the liquid into the pitcher. Dump pulp in trash. Repeat with remaining limes & sugar water.

5) Add sweetened condensed milk. Taste it. If it's bitter just add more sugar and maybe a little more milk.
6) Serve immediately over lots of ice. This does not keep well so don't make this in advance (although you can cut the limes, mix the sugar water and measure the sweetened condensed milk in advance).

Chicken Lasagna

- 2-3 Chicken Breasts
- 2 cans Cream of Chicken
- 1 Cup Sour Cream
- ½ Cup Parmesan Cheese
- ½ teaspoon Garlic Salt
- 2 Cups Mozzarella Cheese
- Onion Salt – to taste
- 9 Lasagna Noodles (Can use zucchini/cucumber noodles for low-Carb)

Chicken Lasagna

Boil chicken and save water to boil lasagna noodles. Make sauce using Cream of Chicken, sour cream, garlic salt & onion salt. Chop chicken into cubes and add to sauce.

Boil noodles about 10-15 minutes until *al dente*. If using Cucumber noodles, use a sheet slicer and pat noodles dry before using.

Layer in a 9x13 cake pan; noodles, sauce, cheese (sprinkle cheeses on each layer of sauce). Do two layers and top with noodles. Add Mozzarella to top layer.

Bake at 350* for approximately 40 minutes covered.

*If you like lots of cheese you can add more Parmesan and Mozzarella to each layer.

Chipped Beef on Toast

- 1 Tablespoon Butter
- ½ Cup Milk
- ¼ Cup Flour
- 1 pkg Corned Beef (Land 'O Frost)
- Peas *optional

Melt butter in saucepan. Mix milk & flour together until all lumps are gone. Heat in saucepan, stirring constantly until thick. If too thick, add more milk. Cut corned beef into pieces and add to pan. Add peas and heat until all is warm. Make some toast. Rip toast into pieces and pour mixture over the toast.

Chimichangas – Lara's

- 2-3 lb Beef Chuck Roast (4-5 lb roast for 6-8 people)
- 1 packet Beefy Onion Soup mix (Lipton)
- Beef-base paste or Beef broth (Use 1 Onion Soup mix with beef base, or 2 Onion Soup mix with 1 can Beef broth)
- 2 – 14 oz. Diced Chili ready Tomatoes (with green chili & onion)
- Chili Powder (coat entire pan – very liberally)
- Cumin (coat entire pan, but not quite as liberally)
- All-Season Salt & Pepper (to taste)
- Cayenne Powder (½ amount of Cumin)
- Extra-large Tortillas
- ½ inch Oil in large skillet

Directions:

Season meat with all-season salt & pepper (liberally). Brown all sides in large skillet before putting in crock pot on low. Add all other ingredients before cooking. If using an oven cook at 225* - 250* for 7 – 10 hours.

After 4 hours, check the meat. Does it shred easily? Shred and taste. You can add more spices if needed. If you want it more spicy add more Cayenne powder. When done, (it is done when meat falls apart) shred the meat & put it back with other ingredients. Bring to a boil (on high) & thicken with cornstarch.

Fan out Extra-large tortillas. Wrap a wet kitchen towel around the tortillas and warm in the microwave for 15 – 30 seconds. Use extra-large tortillas like Don Pancho. Be sure to warm the tortillas before filling & rolling to fry. They don't crack as easily if they are warm.

Put about ½ inch of oil in skillet and turn on burner to high. Wait until oil is hot and ready. Sprinkle water on it. If it splatters/crackles it is ready.

Fill each tortilla with a large spoon of shredded meat, draining excess liquid. Fold both sides & roll tortilla. Fry on both sides until golden brown.

Serve with shredded cheese, shredded lettuce, tomatoes, sour cream & guacamole. Cut long ways down the middle, add toppings & enjoy!

Corn Pudding

- 2 Cans Shoepeg Corn (or sweet white corn)
- 3 Eggs
- 3 Tablespoons Sugar
- ⅓ stick Margarine
- Salt to taste
- Milk

Drain corn. Beat eggs & add to corn. Cover corn with milk. Add sugar & salt. Melt margarine in separate container. Mix everything together & add margarine last.

Bake at 400* about 40 minutes.

Use 1-½ Quart Corningware dish (or 8x8) glass pan.

Cranberry-Orange Pancakes & Syrup

- 1 ½ Cups Low-fat Buttermilk
- ½ Cup Orange Juice
- 2 Eggs
- 1 teaspoon Vanilla
- 1 Cup Wheat Flour
- ¾ Cups All-Purpose Flour
- ¾ Cups Rolled Oats
- ¼ Cup Brown Sugar
- 2 teaspoons Baking Powder
- 1 teaspoon Baking Soda
- ½ teaspoon kosher or Sea Salt
- 1 Cup Cranberries
- 2 Tablespoons Orange Zest (approximately 1 Orange)

*This recipe is best using a Blendtec blender.

Add buttermilk, orange juice, eggs & vanilla to WildSide jar. Secure lid & press Pulse 2-3 times. Add whole wheat flour, all-purpose flour, oats, sugar, baking powder, baking soda & salt to jar. Secure lid & select batter or blend on medium low speed (3-4) for 30 seconds.

Add Cranberries & orange zest to jar. Secure lid & pulse 7 – 10 times or until desired cranberry size is reached. Allow batter to rest 5 minutes.

*You can use French Vanilla Creamer instead of buttermilk. If using creamer, thin out batter with milk.

Citrusy-Cranberry Syrup

- 1 Cup fresh Cranberries
- 2 Oranges, peeled & halved
- ½ Cup Orange Juice
- ⅓ Cup Agave Nectar

Add all ingredients to WildSide jar in order listed. Secure lid & select "whole juice".

Deep Fried French Toast

- 1 Egg
- 1 Cup Flour
- 1 Cup Milk
- ½ Cup Sugar
- 1 Loaf of bread
- ½ inch Oil

French Toast

Combine first 4 ingredients & blend until smooth. Put about ½ inch Oil into electric skillet. Make sure oil is ready by sprinkling water (if it pops & spits, oil is ready). Cover each piece of bread in batter and fry until golden brown on both sides.

You can use croissants for the bread.

Gourmet Grilled Cheese Sandwiches

I have some tips because I finally perfected the Grilled Cheese Sandwich before I was told I am lactose intolerant.

1) Put butter in the skillet (not on the bread) on Medium-Low heat.
2) Put each slice of bread in the skillet and add cheese.
3) Use a lid. This helps trap the heat in and melt the cheese better.
4) If using prosciutto cook in skillet on Medium–low heat prior to use. Once it starts shrinking turn it over to cook on both sides. It only takes about 30 seconds to cook a piece.

Triple "P" Grilled Cheese Sandwich

- Hoagie roll (or bread of choice)
- Pesto (spread on bread)
- Provolone cheese
- Prosciutto (I like to cook prosciutto in large bunches then keep in a Ziploc in the fridge)
- Tomato *optional

Put butter in the skillet and melt on Medium-low heat, put Provolone on both sides of the roll and put in skillet. Add prosciutto. Cover with a lid. Cook until cheese is melted. If using tomato, add before putting the two sides of the roll together. Remove from skillet and enjoy.

Cheddar BBQ Mustard

- Hoagie roll (or bread of choice)
- Smoked Cheddar cheese
- BBQ Mustard sauce
- Prosciutto
- Tomato *optional

Put butter in the skillet and melt on Medium-low heat, put Smoked Cheddar on both sides of the roll and put in skillet. Add prosciutto. Cover with a lid. Cook until cheese is melted. If using tomato, add before putting the two sides of the roll together. Remove from skillet and enjoy.

Varieties:

Colby Jack on one side & Provolone or Swiss on the other. Mix & match the cheeses. You can use various salad dressings or condiments. Be creative.

Jell-O Salad

- 2 Large pkgs (6 oz) Jell-O
- 1 Large Cottage Cheese
- 2 – 8 oz. Whipped topping (or 1 large Whipped topping)
- Fruit

Mix Dry Jell-O, Cottage Cheese & Whipped topping until Jell-O is dissolved. Add drained fruit. Let set in fridge about 1 hour before serving.

Varieties:

- Orange Jell-O, mandarin oranges & pineapple tidbits.
- 1 Strawberry Jell–O & 1 Raspberry Jell-O with mixed berries.

Lobster Bisque Pot Pies

*This recipe makes 6 soup bowl size pot pies.

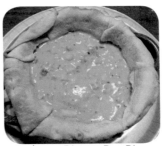
Lobster Bisque Pot Pies

- 3 Containers Pillsbury Crescent Rolls
- 1 Gallon Lobster Bisque Soup (Zupas has it if you can't find any in the store)
- ½ bag Lobster chunk meat
- ½ pkg Frozen Corn
- ½ pkg Southwest style Hash browns (cubed potatoes)
- Milk
- Flour
- 6 Soup Bowls

Spray bowls with non-stick butter.

Roll 2 crescent rolls (with flour) into large flat square/rectangle for each pot pie. Cover base & sides of bowls with rolled dough.

Bake at 350* for 5 minutes.

Pot pie filling:

Thicken lobster bisque with milk & flour (or cornstarch). Add lobster meat chunks, potatoes & corn. Cook until all frozen items are warm.

Put filling in each pot pie. Put flattened crescent rolls on top. Poke holes in top of dough. Bake for 10 minutes (at 350*).

Pasta Salad

- 8 oz. bag Rotini Pasta (zucchini noodles for low-Carb)
- 1 teaspoon Minced Onion
- 1 Yellow Pepper
- 1 Red Pepper
- 1 Cucumber
- 1 can Black Olives (sliced)
- 2 Roma Tomatoes or 1 large tomato
- 1 Cup Bacon Crumbles
- Fat free Italian dressing

Cook pasta with minced Onion until *al dente.* Meanwhile, chop vegetables. Drain pasta when cooked and add all chopped vegetables & bacon crumbles. Add dressing. Chill before serving.

*You can use any vegetables you like. Can use pepperoni and cubed cheddar cheese. Be creative.

Queso

- 1 (12 oz) Can Chili
- 32 oz Velveeta, cubed
- ½ Cup Sour Cream

Queso

Put Chili, Velveeta & Sour Cream in a large bowl.

Microwave 2 minutes. Stir to combine. Continue to microwave 1 minute at a time until melted.

Stovetop: In a large pot combine ingredients, heat and stir until melted.

Crockpot: Combine ingredients, cook on low for 1 hour and stir. If not warm all the way through keep cooking on low.

Red Enchiladas – Open faced

- 8-inch Corn Tortillas
- Oil
- 1 lb Hamburger, browned
- 1 large can Red Enchilada Sauce
- Shredded Cheese
- Shredded Lettuce
- Over-easy egg (1 or 2)

Fry tortillas in oil until crisp. Dip in red enchilada sauce. Layer tortilla with hamburger & shredded cheese. Keep warm in the oven while cooking other layers, & frying eggs. Top with shredded lettuce & fried egg.

Tortilla Soup

- 1 large can Tomato soup (family size)
- 1 can Chicken Broth
- Garlic Powder to taste
- Chili Powder to taste
- Pepper to taste
- Corn tortillas
- 1 lb Browned Hamburger
- Shredded Cheese
- Diced Tomatoes
- Chopped Onion*
- Avocado*

Cut corn tortillas into strips and fry until golden. Combine the first 5 ingredients. Heat in stock pot or large pot on the stove until flavors are blended.

Put fried tortilla strips, browned (cooked) hamburger, shredded cheese and anything else you want in your bowl. Cover with soup & top with Avocado.

Chapter 5: Paradigm Shift

When I went into the doctor for my routine visit, I was told I had borderline diabetes and hypoglycemia. My doctor said if I didn't change my diet, I was in danger of getting full-blown diabetes, and that is much more challenging to manage. She said if I change now, I might not ever get diabetes and I could get to a healthier place.

Now, I've never been the healthiest eater. I enjoy sugar too much (as you can tell from my earlier recipes). I was so good at baking and making sweets, I just fell into a lot of bad eating habits. Even growing up, I was never a skinny girl, but I couldn't lose weight. I tried so many diets and fads, but nothing ever worked. I think I just didn't have the will power to stick with anything. Sugar always drew me back to my bad habits.

In 2010 I had multiple strokes. I have antiphospholipid syndrome. That basically means I have blood-clotting disease. They put me on Warfarin, a blood thinning agent. I was on Warfarin for five years. Anyone who's been on Warfarin knows you need to be consistent with your intake of Vitamin K. This is found in most healthy vegetables, deep leafy greens etc. The easiest way for me to manage my Vitamin K was to have very little to none of it. This also meant that I was not getting the necessary nutrients I needed to digest my foods. I was constantly having cramps and stomach aches. I had to take probiotics before or with every meal so I didn't have stomach issues.

As you can imagine, I was getting frustrated that I was feeling this way all the time. I knew something needed to change. I tried doing some small adjustments, trying to decrease my sugar intake and snack on nuts & dried fruit. That didn't work either. I noticed my kidney started hurting every night after I took my daily dose of Warfarin. I finally switched my blood thinner to Xarelto and did a body cleanse, using smoothies to get the nutrients I needed, to get rid of all the toxins in my body. The great thing is, since Xarelto works differently than Warfarin, I no longer had to monitor my Vitamin K intake, and didn't need to do my monthly INR blood check. I was so excited to eat Vitamin K again. I was like a kid in a candy store, but with vegetables. I think this was the major turning point for me, and I really started liking vegetables again.

When I got the news from my doctor about being pre-diabetic, I wasn't necessarily surprised. I had been getting migraines more frequently. I was tired a lot and felt like I needed a nap just to make it through my day. But, I had so many questions. I had no idea what I was supposed to do and what I could eat.

All of a sudden I was told I could only have 100 grams of Carbohydrates (Carbs) a day, and little to no dairy. My body just doesn't process dairy very well as I get older. What do I do? I hadn't eaten that day, and now I was afraid to eat anything! My sweet husband found a Carb managing App for my phone. I could scan barcodes and search for different foods and find out how many Carbs were in it.

My husband and I went shopping for new low-Carb foods. While at the store, scanning every food, an employee of the store approached us. She talked to us for more than half an hour with helpful tips. Her son is diabetic and she has learned a lot over the years. She was so kind and helpful.

We went to another (warehouse) store and, as you can imagine my blood sugar was very low and I was struggling to walk straight. I started veering right with the shopping cart and ran into my husband. He bumped the cart left to redirect me, and I crashed into the shelves on the left side of the aisle. I just had no strength to control the cart. I was walking very slowly, shuffling my feet. I was struggling getting my leg up to the runner so I could get in the car. It took me at least five attempts just to get in the car. My husband said, "grab your pants and lift your leg." I did that and it worked.

I thought, "This must be what it's like to be drunk." I just move at an extremely slow pace and it's very hard for me to process information – like my brain doesn't work.

That first week was BRUTAL! My energy levels were all over the place, and my stomach and bowels were wreaking havoc. I needed to be close to the bathroom because my body was detoxing and adjusting to new foods. I still wasn't sure what I could eat. One day I would have 30 Carbs, the next I was at 100. I knew meat and vegetables were low in Carbs, but I still didn't want to give up my chocolate. I knew that if I tried to quit cold turkey that I would binge on sweets later. How do I balance my new foods so I could still indulge once in a while?

Finally, I figured out that it was best for me to balance Carbs between my meals. If I had about 30 grams of Carbohydrates per meal, and had healthy snacks at 10:00 and 2:00, I was getting the right balance of energy. For me, it is best that I have vegetables with every meal. If I was lacking the greens my energy would fade quickly. Once my body got used to the new foods, I noticed I didn't need a nap every day. I didn't have the high and low roller coaster energy that I used to. My energy was more mediocre, but consistent all day. It seems as time goes on, my energy is getting better. Now it is more consistent every day and I don't need a nap just to make it through the day. In fact, I only need a nap once or twice a week, depending on life and how much sleep I'm getting at night.

I also talked to my doctor and she said I could have a cheat day, no more than once a week. Also, if I go over my 100 Carbs one day, just eat less Carbs the next day. Try to balance out the week so that I have an average of 100 Carbs a day. That made things easier to manage as well. Also, if I know I'm going to have high Carbs for dinner I can have less Carbs for breakfast and lunch to balance the day.

Luckily, I am blessed with an amazing support system of friends and family who helped me through this difficult time. I learned some amazing cooking methods and ideas for what to eat and not get bored eating the same things. I would like to share everything I have learned so far about healthy eating and new methods to really make cooking easy and fun.

It is best to start making plans for what meals you want to make during the week. I was so used to just grabbing something along the way, but now I need to plan a little better, and figure out what items I need at the store one week at a time. I find I am buying a lot more vegetables, so I need to go to the store more often as vegetables go bad if they're not used. It is good to do smaller trips more often with this way of life so that your vegetables stay good and you don't buy too much. I am working on about one week at a time.

Let's start with tips for breakfast. Now that I wasn't eating cereal and milk every morning I had to find other things to eat. This is where I had to change my idea of what food is considered "breakfast food". Any food is breakfast food, as long as I get the energy and sustenance I need to start the day.

Chapter 6: Transition Tips

Making the transition from high Carbohydrates to healthy eating can be challenging. I hope that this chapter will help if you are going to make a change to low-Carb lifestyle.

Of course, every diet or healthy life style change will be different for each person. Experiment with different foods and pay attention to your body. Some people need to watch their sodium, others cholesterol. I need to watch my dairy intake. I want to share tips and skills I learned that helped me tremendously through this change.

Read labels:

Start reading labels. It will take longer at the store, so plan for it. Look at Carbohydrates in everything you buy. Pay attention to the serving size. A label may say 24 Carbohydrates, but the serving size is 4 pieces. That means one piece only has 6 Carbs. That means you can have that chocolate, but maybe you only want to have one piece so you don't go over your allotted Carbs for the day.

I love to have a smoothie in the morning. I feel like I get good energy after having a smoothie. I was really worried that I wouldn't be able to have smoothies anymore. I used my Carb app to enter the Carbs in each ingredient. I know my blender makes about one gallon. Once I had entered the nutritional facts into "custom foods" I figured out that the amount of smoothie I was consuming was only about 20 – 30 Carbs. Now I love to enjoy a smoothie and a cucumber for breakfast.

I won't claim that what I've done for myself will work for everyone. I'm not a dietician or a nutritionist. These are just a few things that have really helped me. I have learned multiple ways to cook eggs. I have also learned that it is better for me to have vegetables with my breakfast, whether I just have a few small cucumbers and tomatoes, or a smoothie.

Eggs:

Eggs are so versatile. I was really worried at first because I had tried a low Carb/high protein diet when I was in High School. However, I really didn't like different varieties of eggs. I mostly ate scrambled eggs. I was doing scrambled eggs or a diet soda every morning, and I would get sick (to the point of vomiting) about every third day. I was concerned it would be like that again. But, I have learned a variety of ways to cook eggs. I discovered that I really do like different types of eggs. Now that I enjoy cooking, I just need to perfect them the way I like them. Here are some very simple tips in cooking eggs.

Over-easy (or over-medium)

I don't know about you, but I don't like any of the whites of the egg uncooked. I don't like the snotty, slimy egg. I like to use butter to make the pan nice and slippery. Once I crack the egg, I use the spatula to make holes in the thick part so that more egg gets cooked. By putting lines/holes in the bottom I am able cook the whites thoroughly. Then, when I flip it over to the other side, I press down around the yolk for better cooking through the whites.

Now, my over-medium eggs are just about perfect every time.

Hard boiled Eggs

The fastest & easiest way to peel hard boiled eggs is this...once your eggs are done put them in a bowl of ice water for at least 5 minutes. It is easier to peel them if they are cool. Crack the eggshell well before peeling, creating a spiderweb of cracks in the shell. Get the peeling started. Then, you can use a spoon to peel the rest. Just put the spoon between the egg and the shell and circle around the egg.

Deviled Eggs

If you want to do deviled eggs, slice around the yolk and twist the egg whites apart. You can just squeeze the yolk out. If the yolk doesn't pop out, you can use a spoon to scoop it out. I use Miracle Whip and bits of prosciutto or bacon bits. Use a melon baller or small spoon to fill the egg yolks back in. You can sprinkle some paprika on top.

Egg salad is fantastic in a wrap or pita bread with sprouts. Flat bread and some multigrain tortillas are only about 14 – 20 Carbs. Just mix a little mayonnaise (or Miracle Whip) with your chopped up hard-boiled eggs. I like to add bacon bits to this as well.

Egg Tacos

Use 2 eggs in an 8-inch skillet. Break the yolks and cook thoroughly on both sides. Fold to the shape of a taco and fill with toppings: hash browns, cheese, bacon or healthier option prosciutto, cucumbers & tomatoes.

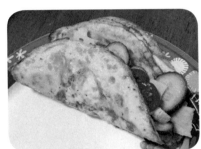

Egg Taco

Smoothies:

I use a Blendtec blender as it really does blend up fruits better than other blenders. Here are my smoothie tips.

1) Use about 16 - 24 oz. of liquid. I like to use juice for extra flavor, but you can use water. Be careful if using juice as most fruit juice is very high in Carbs. I like using drinks with 0 – 8 Carbs for 8 oz. ICE drinks, Vita Rain Water, Clear American ICE, Splash flavored water, or Propel.
2) Add fresh fruits or veggies (about 1 Cup)
3) Add frozen fruits (about 1 Cup)
4) Blend well, add Agave Nectar or French Vanilla creamer for extra sweetness.
5) I mostly use fruits and add a handful of spinach so I get my vegetables. It makes your smoothie color green or brown but doesn't change the taste (unless you add too much). Feel free to add spinach to any of the smoothie recipes for more nutrients.

Here is a list of smoothies I have found or created over the past few years. Many are high in Carbs so you can make substitutions for a healthier version. You can also play with the amounts listed based on the flavor you prefer.

The last few low-Carb recipes were done after we discovered a Farmer's Market with fresh raspberries, blackberries, peaches & nectarines. You can freeze the raspberries & blackberries to use later.

Varities:

Peach, Mango, Grapefruit

- 1 Cup Peach Mango Smoothie Mix (Mango Nectar)
- 2 Cans Peaches
- 1 Grapefruit (peeled and split into pieces)
- 3 Cups Frozen Mangoes

Orange Carrot Smoothie

- ¾ Cup Carrot Juice
- 1 Medium Orange
- ¾ Cup Frozen Mango
- ¾ Cup Pineapple

Caribbean Mix

- Passion Fruit Juice
- 1 pkg Tropical Fruit Mix (frozen – can get at Sam's or Costco)
  - Peach, Mango, Strawberry & Pineapple

*Optional – Agave nectar for sweetness

Triple Berry

- Cran-Tangerine Juice
- Triple Berry Frozen Mix
  - Blackberry, Raspberry, & Blueberry

*Can use different juice, add bananas, or pear

Mint Chocolate Chip

- French Vanilla Creamer
- Agave Nectar
- 1 teaspoon Mint Extract
- 2 big handfuls of spinach
- Add 1 Cup chocolate chips at the very end (only blend about 5 – 10 seconds)

Tang-Carrot Smoothie

- Carrots
- French Vanilla Creamer
- Tang
- Orange Juice
- Agave Nectar

*Can use Orange Cream Smoothie Mix for sweeter smoothie

Strawberry/Banana

- Passion Fruit Juice
- Strawberries (frozen)
- Bananas

Pear Apple Watermelon

- Apple Juice
- 1 Can Pears
- Watermelon

*Can use Banana instead of Watermelon for a completely different smoothie.

Mango-a-go-go

- ½ Cup Mango Nectar
- ½ Cup Orange Juice
- ½ Banana
- 1 Cup Mango
- 2 Cups Strawberries

Powerful Punch

- Pomegranate Juice
- Pineapple
- Peaches
- Pears

Orchard Punch

- Passion Fruit Juice
- Grapefruit
- Orange
- Apples
- Peaches
- Agave Nectar

Strawberry Smash

- 1 Grapefruit
- 4 Oranges
- ½ Banana
- 2-3 Cups Strawberries (frozen)
- French Vanilla Creamer (to taste)

Fruit Flash

- French Vanilla Creamer (to taste)
- Apple Juice
- 2 Cups Peaches
- Mango
- Strawberries
- Spinach

Sunrise Surprise

- Oranges
- Pineapple
- Banana
- Pomegranate Juice

Summer days

- Limonada (24 oz mixed with water until powder dissolves)
- Strawberries
- Watermelon (about 2-3 Cups)
- Mango
- Agave Nectar

Sophisticated Side

- White Cranberry Peach Juice
- 1 Can Peaches
- 1 Can Pears
- 2-3 Cups Watermelon
- Limonada (to taste). Make sure you dissolve in water first.

Mango Blackberry

- Mango Passion Fruit Juice
- 1 Pint (container) Blackberries
- 2-3 Cups Mango
- Agave Nectar

Pomegranate Blackberry

- Pomegranate Juice
- White Cranberry Peach Juice
- French Vanilla Creamer (just a bit – to taste)
- 1 Can Pineapple
- 1 Pint (container) Blackberries
- Strawberries

Morning Twist

- Cran-Tangerine Juice
- 4 Oranges
- ½ Banana
- Strawberries
- Agave Nectar

Peach Passion

- Passion Orange – frozen juice (thaw & add water)
- Peaches

Peach Mango

- Limonada (about 24 oz – make with water & dissolve powder)
- Peaches
- Mango

Overload

- Passion Fruit – frozen juice (thaw & add water)
- Tropical Fruit Mix (Mangoes, Peaches, Pineapple & Strawberries)
- Limonada (with water & dissolved)
- Banana
- Raspberries
- Agave Nectar

Tart & Tangy

- Mango Orange – frozen juice (thaw & add water)
- Raspberries
- Blueberries
- Banana
- Agave Nectar

Watermelon Aqua Fresca

- 24 oz. Limonada (with water & dissolved)
- 2 Cans Frozen Lemonade
- 1 Gallon Size Ziploc bag of frozen Watermelon

Starfruit Sunrise

- ½ Can Pineapple Starfruit juice - frozen juice (thaw & add 16 oz. water)
- 1 Can Pineapple
- ½ Banana
- Mangoes

Peach (My favorite low-Carb smoothie)

- 16 oz Peach I.C.E. (or Clear American ICE)
- 4 – 5 Fresh Peaches

Blackberry Peach

- 16 oz Berry Splash (Flavored water) or Berry Propel
- 1 Pint Blackberries (about 2 Cups)
- 3 – 4 Peaches

Raspberry Nectarine

- 16 oz. Berry Splash or Propel
- 1 Pint Raspberries
- 4 Nectarines

Chapter 7: Low-Carb Tips & Recipes

Here is a quick list of tips to make your transition easier:

1) Stay close to a bathroom the first week or two until your body clears out the toxins.

Your body will start feeling better and you will have less issues as you persist.

2) Keep your Carbs to 100 grams per day on average for the week.

If you go over one day, don't be discouraged and quit. You can just have less Carbs another day. Make sure you are at about 100 grams on average for the week. For example; Monday, I have 110 Carbs, Tuesday I have 90 Carbs, Wednesday I have 50 Carbs, Thursday I have 70 Carbs and Friday I have 130 Carbs. Saturday and Sunday both about 100 Carbs. That means I averaged 92 Carbs a day for the week. Score! No worries. I'm still about 100 Carbs for the week. However, I find that if I shoot for about 30 Carbs each meal I am giving myself the energy I need to make it through the day without crashing. Then, I have Carbs left for a treat at night.

3) You can still have sweets.

There's no way I could give up my chocolate completely. I was also told by my doctor that it's not healthy to stop "cold turkey" because you will binge later, once the craving becomes too strong. Just watch the serving size. My favorite treat at the end of the night is my Intense Dark Chocolate candy bar with fruit (Mango, Raspberry, Orange, etc.). That treat is 24 Carbs per serving. However, a serving size is 3 squares. So, I can have 1 square for 8 Carbs. I have found that if I save my sweet treat for the end of the day I do much better.

Orangeos

At work one day, they were giving out ice cream sandwiches. I didn't want to miss out. So, I had one, and it was big. It was only about 11:00 am. The rest of the day I just wanted to eat ALL DAY! So, I munched on healthy snacks as much as I could, but I noticed I was constantly craving food. My doctor told me if you have sugar first thing in the morning it just perpetuates the constant desire to eat and have more sugar. I have also noticed that if I have a little chocolate early in the day, I crave it more throughout the day. So, if I can resist until after dinner, it is much easier to make it through the day without the constant cravings. I feel like I am rewarding myself at the end of every day when I get to have my little treat. I have found that many of the frozen fruit bars are generally low in Carbs as well. Also, Lindt Lindor truffle balls are approximately 5 Carbs per ball.

4) It is alright to cheat once in a while.

This is a little tricky because you don't want to cheat several days in a row. If you do, this is when you fall off the wagon or feel like you are losing ground. However, let me give you some advice. If you know you are going to cheat for a certain meal, eat very low Carbs on the other meals and snacks that day. If you want to cheat a whole day, you can. Just make sure you ONLY do that once a week.

5) Notice the little things and reward yourself.

When you notice that your pants are a little looser, or that tight shirt fits better, or you can now do your bra up on the inside hooks instead of the outside – rejoice!

Notice everything you possibly can about every little loss of inches or pounds. Even if the scale says you're not losing, notice how your clothes fit, or how you feel.

Reward yourself with a new outfit when you start noticing your current clothes are baggy. It's amazing the boost in self-esteem you receive when you can buy a smaller size.

A few things I started to notice right away: my face and neck were two separate body parts. There was definition around my jaw line. I went from a bra size of 46 DD to 40 B. That was huge! All my pants needed belts, and if I didn't wear belts

Weight loss

they would just hang off my hips. I needed to wear a belt with every pair of pants. When I went to the restroom I didn't need to undo the button or zipper on my pants/shorts.

Also, recognize how you are feeling. My knees didn't hurt as often. I rarely got migraines anymore. I had more consistent long-term energy. It wasn't the roller coaster energy that I had in the past. I didn't need a nap every day just to feel like I could make it. It was amazing the transformation I was feeling. Make sure you acknowledge and recognize yourself for these improvements.

6) Be positive!

If you do get off track don't be discouraged. This is not a trendy diet or something you can do for just a few weeks. You really need to change your lifestyle and commit to this way of life completely. Just remember, this is a healthy way of life, and it will prevent diabetes and other health issues. Foods have the nutrients we need for our bodies to function properly. We just need to eat the right ones.

7) How to overcome the "plateau".

Almost everyone doing a change will hit the plateau. Meaning you just hit a weight and can't seem to lose anymore. It can get you down. This happened to me. About 6 months after I started I had lost 35 pounds, but couldn't seem to get over that hump. I re-evaluated my foods and snacks. I rechecked the Carbs in everything I was eating. I found that I had in my mind that apples were only 16 – 18 Carbs. When I looked it up again, that was only for a small apple. I was eating medium to large apples. Therefore, my snacks were 25 Carbs or more. I was eating about 2 or 3 apples a day. It was my favorite snack.

I cut those down to one a day or every other day. Within a week I lost another 3 pounds. Here is my recommendation if you hit the plateau:

- Re-evaluate what you are eating
- Cut your daily Carb intake to 60 – 70
- Stay on course. If you need to cheat once-in-a-while or have a treat it's still ok. Just stick with it.
- Adjust your foods as needed.

8)   Your loved ones only want you to be healthy and have a long, happy life.

I was talking to my sister about my new healthy lifestyle and she reminded me that she approached me years ago about being healthy. She was worried about my health. She didn't care what size I was. She just noticed a friend's family member having similar issues and was worried I might be in danger. At the time, I was deep in my feelings of hopelessness. I had tried different diets and fads and nothing was working. I felt like I was being judged by her because she approached me.

Now that I am in a better place and working on my health, I had a wonderful conversation with her, and I realized that my point of view back then was very defensive. I believe it was because I was trying so many various things but nothing was working, and I was frustrated. Therefore, I was defensive when anyone mentioned my weight or my health because I felt like they were attacking me, and I wasn't able to do anything to change it.

9)   Count everyday things as exercise.

I only do a few very easy things for exercise. Here are some simple things I do to get my exercise;

- Park at the back of the parking lot when shopping or at work so that I walk just a bit further.
- Take stairs instead of elevators whenever possible.
- Take my dog for a walk.

You may also count chasing your children around the house or the park. Picking up and carrying your child. Count how many times you do the stairs in your house each day. When bringing in groceries you are lifting weights. Think of all the things you do every day that you could turn into exercise.

Rubs & Marinades:

Just because you are going low-Carb doesn't mean you have to eat bland foods or sacrifice taste. Most rubs & marinades are fairly low-Carb. Again, read the label. Marinades or rubs that have more sugar will have more Carbs. Also, remember serving size. You may only be using 3 Tablespoons of the marinade to cover your meat. Take that into consideration when choosing your flavors.

Tips for rubs on different meats:

When using beef or pork coat meat liberally. Put rub or marinade on meat about 30 minutes prior to cooking. The more flavor you want, the longer you should let the meat sit in the flavor before cooking. You can even marinate over-night for deeper flavor.

When using chicken do a light layer of rub. Marinate for 30 minutes – a few hours, no more. If you do marinate over-night the flavor may be too strong.

For seafood, coat very lightly – sprinkle lightly, just before cooking, so your fish is spotted with flavor. If using frozen fish defrost, then sprinkle with rub and use the same day. It will not be good to use after it's been thawed and not used. Fish only takes a few minutes to cook in a skillet or on a BBQ. However, if cooking in the oven it takes longer. Always test with a fork. Once the fish is flaky it's done.

Liquid Marinades:

There are so many delicious marinades out there. Based on the serving size almost all are low-Carb. Make sure to thaw the meat before putting marinade on the meat. You can just use a Ziploc bag to put your meat and marinade. Once sealed move the meat around to make sure all your meat is coated.

When cooking the meat on the BBQ use the extra marinade to baste the meat. Rub on with a brush each time you turn the meat.

When using liquid marinade on fish, do not marinade first. Just cook the fish and spread marinade on during cooking.

Cast Iron Cooking:

I was introduced to Cast Iron cooking and love it! Here are things I've learned in cooking with Cast Iron.

If you have purchased a new Cast Iron Skillet put some oil in it and put it in the oven at 500* for about an hour. Let it cool and wipe out the oil. For best results do not wash your Cast Iron with soap and water. After you cook using a Cast Iron, while it's warm, scrape it out with a metal spatula and wipe it clean with paper towels. The pan will absorb the seasoning you use each time you cook in it. This will make your meat, or whatever you cook in it, taste more flavorful.

Cooking method:

Preheat the oven to 450*. Put a little oil in your Cast Iron pan and put in the oven while it heats. You can either put it in from the start, or wait until your oven reads 250* to put your pan in. Put a little oil in the bottom while heating – just enough to cover the bottom. Once your oven heats to 450* pull your pan out (using hot pads) and add your meat. It will immediately start to sizzle. Be careful of oil spitting. Less oil means less spitting. Change the oven heat to Hi Broil with your oven rack toward the top (I put mine on the second slot). The closer your rack and pan are to the top, the more smoke you will get.

I cook 16 oz. – 20 oz. Ribeye steaks for 8 - 10 minutes on each side for perfectly Medium Well. Steaks are most flavorful if you let them rest 5 – 10 minutes after cooking. Make sure to take them out of the pan and let them rest on a plate before eating or they will continue cooking in the hot pan.

Steak dinner

Depending on the type of meat, how thick it is and how you like it done will determine your cooking time. I have cooked pork, chicken and steak. Drain excess liquid during the cooking process (putting it in a glass jar) for best results. I prefer to do seafood using another method as I do not wash my Cast Iron skillet.

If you marinade your meat with a liquid do not add the rest of the liquid to the pan while cooking the meat. It will cook right into the pan and becomes very difficult to clean. If you do run into this situation you can soak the pan in hot water and then scrape it out.

Asparagus – Grilled Parmesan

- Asparagus
- Extra Virgin Olive Oil
- Parmesan Cheese (shredded)

Put about 40 asparagus spears in a gallon Ziploc bag. Pour in some Olive Oil. Toss until all spears are coated. Grill on medium heat about 5 minutes. Add Parmesan cheese and serve. *You can put the asparagus, oil & cheese in aluminum foil to cook on the BBQ or use a grill plate. You can add the cheese after if not using foil.

Asparagus – Roasted with Balsamic Browned Butter

- 40 Asparagus Spears
- Cooking Spray
- ¼ teaspoon Kosher Salt
- ¼ teaspoon freshly ground Black Pepper
- 2 Tablespoons Butter
- 2 teaspoons low-sodium Soy Sauce
- 1 teaspoon Balsamic Vinegar
- Cracked Black Pepper *Optional
- Grated Lemon Zest *Optional

1) Preheat oven to 400*
2) Arrange asparagus in a single layer on a baking sheet; coat with cooking spray. Sprinkle with salt and pepper. Bake at 400* for 12 minutes or until tender.
3) Melt butter in a small skillet over medium heat; cook 3 minutes or until lightly browned, shaking pan occasionally. Remove from heat; stir in soy sauce and balsamic vinegar. Drizzle over asparagus, tossing well to coat. Garnish with cracked pepper and lemon rind if desired.

Asparagus & Ham

- Asparagus
- Ham (Lunch meat or deli sliced)
- Cream Cheese *Optional

Cut ham in half. Spread a little cream cheese and wrap raw asparagus. Use a toothpick to hold it together. This makes a great appetizer. You can leave out the cream cheese if you are watching your dairy intake.

Avocado Chocolate Mousse

- 1 Ripe Avocado – halved, peeled & seeded
- ½ Cup Cocoa Powder
- 1 Tablespoon Vanilla
- ½ Cup Agave Nectar
- ¼ Cup Coconut Milk
- ¼ Cup Sliced Strawberries

Mousse

Chop Avocado into a few pieces and put in food processor. Can use the small Blendtec jar. Avacodo should be smooth.

Add Cocoa Powder, Vanilla, Agave Nectar & Coconut Milk and blend well, until mousse reaches desired consistency. I use a hand mixer. If you want less bitter chocolate use half the cocoa.

Chill & serve with berries.

One large avocado averages about an 8 oz. serving.

Blackberry Pork – slow cooker

- 2 lb Pork Tenderloin
- 1 teaspoon Salt
- 1 teaspoon Black Pepper
- 1 Tablespoon Dried Rubbed Sage
- 1 Tablespoon Crushed Dried Rosemary
- 16 oz. jar Seedless Blackberry jam
- ¼ Cup Honey
- 2 Tablespoons Dry Red Wine (can use grape juice)

Blackberry Pork

Sauce:

- ½ Cup Red Wine
- 2 Tablespoons Honey
- 1 Cup fresh Blackberries

Season pork on all sides with salt, pepper, sage & Rosemary. Place pork in slow cooker, and spoon jam, ¼ Cup Honey & 2 Tablespoons Red Wine over pork.

Set on low for 4-5 hours.

About 15 minutes before serving time, pour ½ cup Red Wine, 2 Tablespoons Honey & fresh Blackberries into a sauce pan. Bring to a boil over medium-low heat, and simmer until sauce thickens slightly & some berries burst, about 15 minutes.

Serve pork in slices, and drizzle sauce over before serving.

*You can use raspberries instead, but it will be more of a compote sauce with less full berries.

Blackberry Salmon

- ½ Cup Seedless Blackberry Jam
- 3 Tablespoons Red Wine Vinegar
- 1 Salmon fillet (2 ¼ lb), thawed if frozen, cut into 6 (6 oz.) pieces
- Olive Oil Cooking Spray
- 1 Tablespoon Lemon-Pepper Seasoning Salt
- 1 Cup Fresh Blackberries

1) Heat gas or charcoal grill. In 1-quart saucepan, cook jam and vinegar over medium heat 2 to 3 minutes, stirring constantly, until jam is melted. Remove from heat; set aside.
2) Spray both sides of salmon pieces with cooking spray. Rub lemon-pepper seasoning salt over both sides of salmon. Place large sheet of heavy-duty foil on grill rack over medium heat. Place salmon, skin sides down, on foil. Cover grill; cook 8 - 10 minutes or until fish flakes easily with a fork. Remove from heat.
3) Serve salmon topped with blackberry glaze & berries.

Varieties:

You can use any seedless jam or syrup for different flavors. For example, Apricot Syrup with Apple Cider Vinegar over pork tenderloin.

Notes:

To make your glaze thicker, mix some cornstarch with warm water until all lumps are gone. Add to jam and mix over heat. Constantly stir until you reach the thickness you desire.

Broccoli Salad

Broccoli Salad

- ½ Cup Bacon Crumbles or 6 slices of cooked and crumbled Bacon
- 3 Chopped Broccoli heads (about 6 – 8 Cups)
- ½ Cup Sunflower Seeds

Dressing:

- 1 Cup Mayonnaise (or Miracle Whip)
- 2 Tablespoons Red Wine Vinegar
- ½ Cup Sugar

Mix until smooth

Toss all ingredients together. Add dressing just before serving. You may also add Craisins.

Buffalo Chicken Dip

Buffalo Chicken Dip

- 4 Chicken Breasts – boiled and shredded, or you can use 3 cans of chicken.
- 12 oz. bottle of Frank's Original Hot Sauce (use only half the bottle if you don't want it spicy, or use extra Ranch).
- 1 Cup Ranch dressing
- 8 oz. Cream Cheese
- 1 Cup (8 oz.) Shredded Sharp Cheddar Cheese

After you boil & shred chicken (or just add canned chicken), combine all ingredients in a crock pot. Cook 1 hour stirring occasionally. Then keep on warm until serving.

Cabbage Salad

- 1 Head White Cabbage
- 1 Can Pineapple (Crushed or Tidbits)
- 1-2 Bananas
- 1 Cup Mayonnaise (or Miracle Whip)

Shred Cabbage and drain juice from pineapple. Save the pineapple juice in a cup. Add pineapple and sliced bananas. Mix 1 Cup Mayonnaise and about ½ Cup Pineapple juice until smooth. Pour over salad until everything is nicely coated.

Carrot Salad

- 3 – 4 Carrots – grated
- 2 – 3 Apples – grated
- Approximately ⅓ Cup Lemon juice
- Sugar – to taste

Add shredded Carrots & Apples together. It should be a nice even amount of both. Add lemon juice and sugar to taste. Salad should be sweet, but not too sugary.

Chicken Salad

(Watch serving size as this is a little higher in Carbs)

- 1 Can Chicken Breast or 1 cooked and shredded chicken breast
- 2 Apples
- 3 – 4 Celery stalks
- 1 Cup Mayonnaise (or Miracle Whip)
- ½ Cup Fruit juice
- Grapes or Craisins

Cut Apples & Celery into small pieces. Add Chicken, Apples, Celery and Grapes together so there is a nice mix of each ingredient. Blend Mayonnaise & Fruit Juice until smooth. Pour over the other ingredients so everything is coated.

Chicken – Slow Cooker

- 8 oz. Cream Cheese – softened
- 1 Can Cream of Chicken soup (Cream of mushroom works as well)
- 1 pkg dry Zesty Italian Dressing (regular Italian is ok too)
- 4 Large Chicken Breasts

Combine first 3 ingredients in crockpot & mix well. Nestle chicken in mixture. Cook on high for 4 hours. Shred chicken & mix with sauce until all chicken is coated.

Best served over rice. For low-Carb option use Cauliflower rice. Cook with Chicken stock.

Chili Lime Marinade

- ¼ Cup Fresh Lime Juice
- 2 Tablespoons Cilantro or Parsley
- 1 Tablespoon Thai Sweet Chili Sauce
- 2 Garlic Cloves finely chopped (or 2 Tablespoons minced Garlic)
- ½ Tablespoon Honey
- Pinch of Salt

Varieties:

Mahi Mahi - use an 8 x 8 glass pan. Marinade 15 – 30 minutes on each side before baking.

Bake at 325* for 20 minutes. Turning over halfway through. If not flaky after 20 minutes bake another 3 – 5 minutes uncovered.

Chicken – Marinade for 1 – 2 hours before baking.

You can also just cook on a BBQ or in a skillet.

Cucumber Noodles

If you have a Kitchen Aid you can get a Spiralizer attachment. This allows you to make noodles out of Zucchini or Cucumbers. Since my husband doesn't like Zucchini, we have been doing this with Cucumbers and found some fabulous recipes and pasta dishes are back on the menu – using Cucumber noodles instead of pasta.

Tips for Cucumber noodles:

Once you have made the noodles, wash and drain out excess moisture. Pat dry with paper towels before using.

Peanut Sauce

- ⅔ Cup Creamy Peanut Butter
- 2 Tablespoons Rice Vinegar
- 2 ½ Tablespoons Soy Sauce
- 2 teaspoons Sesame Oil
- 2 teaspoons Agave Nectar
- 1 teaspoon Fresh Lime Juice
- 1 Clove or 1 Tablespoon Minced Garlic
- 1 teaspoon Finely grated Ginger (or Ginger Powder)
- Dash of Red Pepper Flakes to taste
- ⅓ Cup Warm Water
- Chopped Peanuts (to taste)

Cucumber salad

In large bowl, combine all ingredients. Add water and whisk until smooth. Add chopped nuts for crunch.

*This is excellent with Cucumber noodles as a salad.

Chicken Lasagna with Cucumber Noodles

Cucumber Chicken Lasagna

- 2-3 Chicken Breasts
- 2 cans Cream of Chicken
- 1 Cup Sour Cream
- ½ Cup Parmesan Cheese
- ½ teaspoon Garlic Salt
- 2 Cups Mozzarella Cheese
- Onion Salt – to taste
- 1 English Cucumber – make noodles

Cut chicken into cubes and boil. Use spiralizer or sheet slicer to make cucumber into noodles. Rinse & drain excess liquid from noodles and pat dry. Make sauce using cream of chicken, sour cream, garlic salt & onion salt. Add chicken to sauce.

Layer in a 9x13 cake pan; cucumber noodles, sauce, cheese (sprinkle cheeses on each layer of sauce). Layer noodles on the bottom of the pan. Spread chicken & sauce over the noodles. Sprinkle with parmesan & mozzarella cheese. Add another layer of cucumber noodles, chicken & sauce, and sprinkle with cheese.

Bake at 350* for approximately 40 minutes covered. Lasagna is done when all cheese is melted on top.

*You can add one more layer of cucumber to the top if you like and top with cheese only. If you like lots of cheese you can add more Parmesan and Mozzarella to each layer.

Egg & Green Bean breakfast

- Green Beans
- Prosciutto/Bacon
- Eggs

Egg & Green Bean Breakfast

Steam the green beans. I use a steamer, put just a bit of water in the bottom, and put in the microwave for 1-2 minutes (about 10-15 beans per person). Put green beans on a plate and sprinkle the top with bacon bits or prosciutto. Top with two over-medium eggs. You can do this with asparagus & bacon or any substitutes you want.

*For extra flavor, make with 1 Teriyaki chicken breast and add some honey mustard.

Fried Cauliflower Rice

- 1 Head Cauliflower, grated
- ¼ - ½ Cup Soy Sauce
- 3 Eggs
- 1 Cup chopped Carrots
- ½ - 1 Cup Peas
- ½ - 1 Cup Ham, cubed

Cauliflower Rice

In a Wok skillet, put oil in and warm the pan. Scramble the eggs. Add grated cauliflower & other ingredients. Stir and cook, mixing all ingredients. Once all cauliflower is coated with Soy Sauce and all is heated you are ready to serve.

Garlicky Lemon Mahi Mahi

- 3 Tablespoons Butter, divided
- 1 Tablespoon Extra-Virgin Olive Oil
- 4 Mahi Mahi fillets (4 oz each)
- Kosher Salt
- Freshly ground Black Pepper
- 3 Cloves Garlic, minced (or 3 Tablespoons)
- Zest & juice of 1 Lemon
- 1 Tablespoon Freshly chopped Parsley, plus more for garnish

Garlicky Lemon Mahi Mahi

1) In a large skillet over medium heat, melt 1 Tablespoon butter & olive oil. Add Mahi Mahi & season with salt & pepper. Cook until golden, 3 minutes per side. Transfer to a plate.
2) To skillet, add remaining 2 Tablespoons butter. Once melted, add garlic and cook until fragrant, 1 minute, then stir in lemon zest & juice & parsley. Return Mahi Mahi fillets to skillet & spoon over sauce.
3) Garnish with more parsley & serve.

Guacamole

- 5-6 Large Avocados (ripe)
- ⅓ Cup Medium Salsa (Pace Picante)
- ½ Cup Sour Cream
- Garlic Salt (to taste about ½ teaspoon)
- Black Pepper (to taste about ½ teaspoon)
- All-Season Salt (to taste about ½ teaspoon)
- 1 Tablespoon Lemon Juice

Cut, peel & remove the seed from the Avocados, and put in a mixer. Add other ingredients and mix together well. Adjust seasoning to taste if needed. Keep one Avocado pit in guacamole after prepared. It will keep it green longer.

Halibut Casserole

- Halibut (about 1 lb)
- All-Season Salt (Johnny's)
- 1 Cup Grated cheese (or enough to sprinkle over halibut)
- 1 Cup Mayonnaise (or Miracle Whip)
- White Pepper

*Cooked shrimp or crab – optional

Sprinkle white pepper on the bottom of a 9x9 Pyrex or glass cake pan. Cut halibut into pieces. Mix mayonnaise & grated cheese. Start with 1 Cup. The mixture should be the consistency of peanut butter. Use as much is needed to cover the halibut. *If using shrimp or crab, layer on halibut before covering with mayonnaise & cheese.

Bake uncovered at 375* for 20 minutes or until halibut is flaky. If not flaky, cook another 5 minutes.

Honey Cashew Nut Butter

- 1 ½ Cups Honey Cashews

Put Cashews in the Twister jar if using a Blendtec (blender). Blend on Power 7 (high) for 50 seconds constantly turning the Twister jar lid.

Key Lime Pie – No bake (Gluten-free, guilt-free)

Crust:

- 2 Cups Almond Flour
- ⅓ Cup Coconut Oil (melted)
- 3 Tablespoons Erythritol (organic sweetener)

Key Lime Pie

Pie filling:

- 2 Medium Avocados
- 12 oz Cream Cheese (softened at room temperature or by heating)
- 4 Small Limes
- 1 Cup Powdered Erythritol (put in blender on high until ground into powder)
- 1 teaspoon Vanilla

1) Line the bottom of a pie pan with parchment paper (optional, but makes it easier to remove later).
2) To make the crust, stir together the almond flour, coconut oil & erythritol. Press the crust into pie pan. Set aside or put in fridge.
3) Place Avocado (skin removed), softened cream cheese, erythritol and vanilla into high powered blender (or use hand mixer) or food processor.
4) Zest Limes & add zest to blender. Squeeze juice out of all Limes and add juice to blender (about 1 Cup). Puree mixture until smooth, scraping down the sides with a spatula.
5) Pour/spoon mixture into the crust. Smooth with spatula or back of spoon.
6) Refrigerate for at least 2 hours, until pie is firm.

*You can use 3 limes if you don't want it too tart, or add more (¼ Cup) powdered Erythritol to cut tartness.

Lamb Chops (Rosemary & Garlic)

- 1 lb Lamb Chops
- 2 Tablespoons Rosemary
- 2 teaspoons Salt
- 1 teaspoon Pepper
- 1 heaping teaspoon Minced Garlic
- 4 Tablespoons Olive Oil (Divided)

Lamb Chop dinner

In a small bowl mix Rosemary, Salt, Pepper, Garlic and 2 Tablespoons Olive Oil. Rub mixture on each chop. Let marinade for 30 – 45 minutes.

In a skillet heat 2 Tablespoons Olive Oil over high heat. When oil is simmering hot, sear chops on all sides about 2 – 3 minutes per side.

Put in oven at 400* for another 5 minutes (for Medium-Well) or until cooked to your liking in the middle.

Test for doneness (internal temperature 165*). Then, cover with foil & let sit for 5 minutes before serving.

Lobster Tacos – Red

- 1 jar Red Guajillo Chile Sauce (Herdez)
- Salsa – Store made Mild (small container)
- Tomatoes
- 1 bag Lobster chunk meat

Toppings:

- Shredded Cheese
- Shredded Lettuce
- Avocado/guacamole
- 8-inch Tortillas

Chop meat into small pieces – rinse and drain all excess water. Warm lobster meat in a skillet (should already be cooked) with a little oil.

While lobster is warming, combine Guajillo sauce, salsa & 2 tomatoes (or to preference) in a bowl.

Once lobster meat is warm, add meat to mixture.

Fill tortilla with meat mixture & shredded cheese. Cook in skillet on both sides until cheese is melted and a nice crisp color is on the tortilla.

Add shredded cheese, chopped tomatoes, shredded lettuce & guacamole.

Lobster Tacos – Chili Lime

- ¼ Cup Fresh Lime Juice
- 2 Tablespoons Olive Oil
- 1 Tablespoon Cilantro or Parsley
- 2 Tablespoons Thai Sweet Chili Sauce
- 2 Garlic Cloves finely chopped (or 2 Tablespoons minced Garlic)
- ½ Tablespoon Honey
- Pinch of Salt
- 8-inch tortillas

Lobster Taco

Toppings

- Shredded Cabbage
- Shredded Cheese
- Chopped tomatoes or mild salsa

Marinade lobster meat overnight. Heat lobster meat in a skillet with marinade. Cook tortillas in a little oil (about 15 seconds on each side). Fold and fill tortilla with lobster meat & shredded cheese. Add desired toppings.

Lobster Tails

- 3 – 4 Lobster Tails
- All season salt

Prepare Lobster:

To prepare Lobster Tails for cooking, use kitchen shears to cut down the middle of the back to the last section. Then, cut to each side – make a "T" down the tail. Squeeze legs together so the meat is showing. Sprinkle meat with All-Season Salt.

Cooking Directions:

Use a Pasta pot with basket. Bring water to a boil. Place tails in basket so they are sitting above the water. Steam approximately 3 - 7 minutes until shell is red.

Serving Directions:

Squeeze legs together under the lobster tail, and pull meat out of the cut. Place meat on top of the shell and sprinkle with more salt if needed. Serve with Garlic Butter and steamed vegetables.

Maple Bacon Wrapped Scallops

- ¾ Cups Maple Syrup
- ¼ Cup Low Sodium Soy Sauce
- 1 Tablespoon Dijon Mustard
- 12 slices of bacon (halved)
- 24 toothpicks
- 2 Tablespoons Brown Sugar

Surf 'N Turf

Directions:

1) Stir together Syrup, Soy Sauce, and Dijon Mustard until smooth. Add scallops and toss to coat. Cover bowl with plastic wrap & marinade at least 1 hour.
2) Pre-heat oven to 375*. Line a rimmed baking sheet with foil.
3) Arrange bacon pieces on baking sheet so they don't overlap. Bake in oven until some of the grease has rendered out of the bacon; the bacon should be soft and pliable, about 8 minutes. Remove bacon from baking sheet & pat with paper towels to remove excess grease. Drain or wipe grease from baking sheet.
4) Wrap each scallop with a piece of bacon and secure with a toothpick. Place onto baking sheet. Sprinkle the scallops with brown sugar.
5) Bake in oven until the scallops are opaque and the bacon is crisp, 10 – 15 minutes, turning once.

Mushrooms – Sauteed

- 1 Container Mushrooms (8 oz)
- ½ Cup Bacon crumbled (bacon bits, or pork belly)
- 1 Tablespoon Butter
- 1 Clove Garlic (or 1 Tablespoon Minced Garlic)

Put Butter in a large skillet (or Wok skillet), add garlic, mushrooms and cooked bacon. Mix in skillet until all butter is melted and ingredients are hot. This is an excellent topping for Cast Iron steaks.

Sauteed Mushrooms

Pot Roast – Slow Cooker

- 3 – 4 pounds Beef Roast
- 1 packet Lipton Onion Soup Mix
- 2 Cups Water
- Baby Carrots
- Potatoes

Mix 2 Cups warm Water with Lipton Onion Soup Mix. Put Roast, Carrots & Potatoes in Crock Pot and cover with mixture. Cook on low about 4 hours until veggies are soft and meat is done.

Teriyaki Marinade

- 1 Cup Soy Sauce
- ⅓ Vegetable Oil/Olive Oil
- 4 oz. Pineapple juice
- ¼ Cup Brown Sugar
- ⅓ Cup Water
- 1 Tablespoon Minced Onions
- Garlic Salt to taste (about 1 teaspoon)

Put all ingredients together in a Ziploc bag and mix well. Marinade 1-2 pounds of chicken or other meat for several hours or overnight.

Tzatziki (Cucumber dip)

- ½ Large Cucumber, unpeeled
- 1 ½ Cups Plain Greek Yogurt
- 2 Large Garlic Cloves finely minced (or 2 Tablespoons minced Garlic)
- 2 Tablespoons Extra Virgin Olive Oil
- 1 Tablespoon White Vinegar
- ½ teaspoon Salt
- 1 Tablespoon Minced Fresh Dill

Tzatziki

1) Grate cucumber & drain through a fine mesh sieve overnight in the fridge. Put on top of a bowl to catch excess liquid.
2) Combine yogurt, garlic, oil, vinegar & salt in a large bowl. Cover & refrigerate overnight.
3) Transfer the grated cucumber & fresh dill to the yogurt mixture & stir to combine.

Serve chilled with vegetables, pita bread or use as sandwich sauce.

Waldorf Salad

- 2 Apples
- 3 – 4 Celery stalks
- 1 Cup Mayonnaise (or Miracle Whip)
- ½ Cup Fruit juice
- Raisins
- Walnuts   *Optional

Cut Apples & Celery into small pieces. Add Apples, Celery and Raisins together so there is a nice mix of each ingredient. Blend Mayonnaise & Fruit Juice until smooth. Pour over the other ingredients so everything is coated.

Chapter 8: Low-Carb Snacks

I have had many people approach me about my new healthy lifestyle because it is working so well for me. It was suggested that I make a list of healthy snacks and where to find them. These are just ideas and things I have found that I like. Below is a quick reference list:

- Veggie Straws (Sam's Club or Costco)
- Skinny Pop popcorn (Sam's Club or Costco)
- Nuts (Almonds, Macadamia nuts, Peanuts, Cashews) – just watch the number of Carbs per serving size.
- Vegetables are generally low in Carbs, but watch the fruits as they have natural sugars (fructose).
- Cucumbers & Guacamole (I like this for breakfast)
- Green Beans
- Carrots & Ranch dressing or Tzatziki
- Cherry/Grape tomatoes
- Apples & Peanut Butter (be careful with apples as they are a bit high in Carbs. Limit yourself to one apple per day).
- Celery & Peanut Butter (or I like to make my own honey cashew nut butter)
- Celery & Buffalo Chicken Dip
- Rice logs (I like those with honey cashew nut butter too)
- Flat bread is a good substitute for bread. You can find this at Harmon's, Smith's and Walmart. They are 14 – 20 Carbs per piece as opposed to bread that is usually 25 Carbs per piece. I have found "Flat Out" and "Joseph's" brands taste best.
- Asparagus & Ham
- Fritos/Cheetos – single size snack bag is about 16 Carbs
- Eggs – all varieties (just keep your cholesterol in check)
- Jerky – Beef, pork and chicken; all varieties are low in Carbs. Sweet flavors will be higher in Carbs.
- Fruit leather – check the Carbs

Celery & Nut butter

Here are some alternative options for energy, caffeine and dairy:

Zipfizz is my energy drink – mix with about 16 oz of water. Natural energy with lots of vitamins & only 2 Carbs. This helps my eyes if they are tired or stressed, and seems to help my headaches ease.

Natural forms of Caffeine – if you need to stop a headache: Coconut milk, Green Tea or Zipfizz

Emergen-C – if you need a boost of vitamins this is good as well. About 8 Carbs per packet

Dairy Substitutes:

Coconut milk, Almond Milk & other types of nut milk are good substitutes for dairy

Ice Cream – Cold Treat options:

Nada Moo – non-dairy ice cream made with coconut milk.

Acai Berry Bites (Sam's Club) - 8 Carbs

Fruit Bars

Smoothie bars or smoothies

Remember, many things can be a good snack, just watch the Carbs per serving and eat according to the amount of Carbs you want to use for the day.

Chapter 9: Transition Phases

1) Exploratory Stage – get started.

This is the beginning stage. You need to have the desire to start making changes. You can take smaller steps, like I did, eating healthier snacks like apples and peanut butter. This really helped me make a change and I still felt like I was having something sweet. I probably ate 3 – 4 apples a day (which is way too much), but it started me on a healthier path, and I still lost 20 pounds this way. You can have a nectarine or plum or peach as a dessert. I have been doing this and I'm losing more.

Track EVERYTHING, meals, snacks, drinks, etc. Keep track of every single thing you partake of, so you count every little Carb and get used to balancing out your day.

Keep high Carb foods and snacks away! You don't need the temptation. It is easier to be good when you don't have a chocolate bar in the cupboard calling your name. Keep a low-Carb sweet available to reward yourself at the end of every day. I had a Lindt Lindor truffle (about 5 Carbs) to end my day. Savor it. Eat it slowly and in small bites.

Your energy levels might be up and down during this stage as you get accustomed to new foods and how much you can have. My energy was somewhat low, but consistent.

I noticed changes in my digestion. I didn't need to have probiotics before or with every meal like I did before. Less stomach cramps and random aches. My headaches started lessening.

During this Stage I didn't think I would ever bake again. Everything I made was high in Carbs and sugar. I didn't do any sweet recipes or baking during this time. I focused on new recipes and new ways of cooking and making healthy meals.

2) Finding your groove.

This stage is when you will start to be comfortable with your foods. You have now been tracking everything and know what foods are low-Carb and it is easier to balance your Carbs throughout the day.

This may be when you hit the "plateau". Now you are comfortable with your foods you don't need to track everything so closely. You can estimate. However, this is a good time to re-evaluate your snacks and any foods you think may be keeping you from continuing your weight loss.

This is where I felt stuck. I hit the plateau and was getting frustrated. I re-evaluated and cut apples out of my daily snack routing. I started snacking on plums, peaches and nectarines as they are lower in Carbs than apples. I found that by doing this I no longer needed my chocolate treat at the end of the night. I didn't crave it.

If you are feeling like you hit that plateau, cut your intake to 60 – 70 Carbs per day for a little while. I did this and noticed within a week I had lost another 3 pounds and was back on track and feeling positive about my lifestyle again.

3) Ride the high.

Now you should be feeling confident in your food choices. You have celebrated every success, every pound lost, every inch and noticed your improved energy levels. You are proud of yourself for the progress you've made, and feel this could really be a permanent lifestyle for you now.

This is where I am now. I feel like I have come full circle with my weight loss challenges. I now know how to have delicious foods and prepare good meals. I am no longer tempted by all that sugar.

I am now able to bake again and not be tempted by it. In fact, I notice how different my mind-set is. As I am baking now, I notice how much sugar I am putting in a recipe and it surprises me. It's nice that I know I can have a taste of whatever I am making (to make sure it tastes good) and it's not going to kill my Carbs for the day. Then, I feel like I have had my fill of sweets.

Now, I am selling my baked goods so I can publish this book. It can be a little challenging as the more I bake the more tempting it is. So, finding a balance is the key.

Chapter 10: Conclusion

I just want to wrap up this book by encouraging you to be creative with your foods. Any food can be eaten any time of the day. Change your way of thinking if you are stuck. Follow your guidelines to be healthy. You can adjust the number of Carbs you have in a day based on personal needs. Don't be afraid to experiment with recipes and foods. As you do this more often your tastes will develop, and you'll start to discover that you can put flavors together and create something amazing.

I truly believe that you must have a desire to change your lifestyle, not just try some fad or diet, to really make a positive change in your life and be the healthy person you want to be. It can be very challenging as we all have beliefs and ideas that get cemented in our minds. I thought I would never be able to make a major change like this to my life. But, when I found out my health was in danger and I could be looking at insulin and a forced change for the rest of my life, I All of a sudden had that desire that drove me to success. I am still a work in progress. Now, I celebrate every little success in losing weight or noticing my clothes are bigger. It inspires me to keep it up and continue being healthy. In fact, I find that when I eat more Carbs or sugar my body doesn't like it. I get cramps and don't feel well if I have too much. Then, I feel more inclined to eat better the next day to make up for it. I now have a deep desire to be healthy. I like the way it feels and want to be this way the rest of my life.

I have been blessed to figure all this out so quickly, as this can be such a difficult concept to put into action. I have been living this new lifestyle a year now, but I have seen some amazing changes, and the factors that lead to diabetes are fading from my body. I am completely free from pre-diabetic factors now. However, I plan on living my life according to this system of a low-Carb, low dairy diet. Now that I am comfortable with foods, I don't track my Carbs on my App. However, I am constantly keeping in mind the amount of Carbs I've had for the day. I find that I am much happier and healthier every day and I plan on keeping it that way. This was a life lesson I had to learn to get my weight and health in check. Now that I am in control, I want to help others do the same. I hope this book will inspire you and help you make some changes too. If that is not what you want to get from this book, just enjoy some good recipes. ☺

It is ironic that to publish my book I am selling all my baked goods to raise the money. Selling the unhealthy/sweet treats so I can help others be healthy and change their lives. However, I feel like it is a means to an end. It took seven months to raise the money I need to publish. Now, I can focus on helping people be healthy.

Index

Printed in the United States
By Bookmasters